The Ultimate Business Plan

Three Week Loan
Benthyciad Tair Wythnos

This item should be returned or brought in for renewal by the last date stamped below.

Time-saving books that teach specific skills to busy people, focusing on what really matters; the things that make a difference – the *essentials*. Other books in the series include:

Selling Your Home Using Feng Shui

Writing Good Reports

Speaking in Public

Responding to Stress

Succeeding at Interviews

Solving Problems

Hiring People

Getting Started on the Internet

Writing Great Copy

Making the Best Man's Speech

Making Great Presentations

Making the Most of Your Time

For full details please send for a free copy of the latest catalogue. See back cover for address.

The things that really matter about

The Ultimate Business Plan

Phil Stone

ESSENTIALS

Published in 2000 by
How To Books Ltd, 3 Newtec Place,
Magdalen Road, Oxford OX4 1RE, United Kingdom
Tel: (01865) 793806   Fax: (01865) 248780
e-mail: info@howtobooks.co.uk
www.howtobooks.co.uk

British Library Cataloguing in Publication Data.
A catalogue record for this book is available from
the British Library.

Edited by Julie Nelson
Cover design by Shireen Nathoo Design
Produced for How To Books by Deer Park Productions
Typeset by PDQ Typesetting, Newcastle-under-Lyme, Staffordshire
Printed and bound by Hillman Printers, Frome, Somerset

NOTE: The material contained in this book is set out in good faith for
general guidance and no liability can be accepted for loss or expense
incurred as a result of relying in particular circumstances on
statements made in the book. Laws and regulations are complex
and liable to change, and readers should check the current position
with the relevant authorities before making personal arrangements.

ESSENTIALS *is an imprint of*
How To Books

Contents

Preface   7

1   Before you start   **9**

Understanding the business plan concept   10

Understanding why you need a business plan   10

Establishing the purpose   12

Knowing who to involve   13

Considering confidentiality   14

2   Doing your research   **17**

Using a SWOT analysis   18

Using a PESTE analysis   18

Finding out about your competitors   21

Considering existing resources   22

Using analysis of past performance   23

3   Evaluating all the options   **26**

Assessing your options   27

Are they suitable?   28

Assessing their feasibility   29

Are they acceptable?   30

4   Formulating the strategy   **33**

Defining your business goals   34

Considering the marketing strategy   35

Identifying any additional resources   37

Constructing the financial forecasts   39

5   Constructing the business plan   **41**

The all-important synopsis   42

Keeping it simple   43

Using fact not fiction   44

Telling the truth   44

What to include   45

What not to include   46

6   **Review and start the process again**   **48**

Reviewing performance against budgets   49

Managing risk   50

Management information   51

Staying ahead of the competition   52

Appendix A: Sample business plan template   **55**

Appendix B: Useful contacts   **62**

Preface

Every aspect of life requires a plan of one sort or another, whether it is simply going to the shop to purchase food, or making sure you have enough fuel in your car to reach your destination. Running your own business is no different. You must plan your objectives, research your route, make sure you have adequate resources, and then finally plan your strategy. Only then will you stand any chance of success.

Success in business does not come easily. It will only come with hard work and planning. All too often, however, planning is left aside and only undertaken when something goes wrong. If a business plan had been compiled at the outset it might have identified potential problems before they occurred and provided an opportunity to avoid them.

This book will help you with all the aspects of writing your business plan. If you follow the techniques for preparation and research and formulate your strategies, you will be able to compile a business plan to run your business more effectively. Do not forget: writing your business plan is only the start. Business planning is a constant cycle, you can never reach the end.

Phil Stone

1 Before You Start

A business plan is a vital tool for all businesses.
Fail to plan and you plan to fail.

5 things that really matter

1 **UNDERSTANDING THE BUSINESS PLAN CONCEPT**

2 **UNDERSTANDING WHY YOU NEED A BUSINESS PLAN**

3 **ESTABLISHING THE PURPOSE**

4 **KNOWING WHO TO INVOLVE**

5 **CONSIDERING CONFIDENTIALITY**

Many business owners see a **business plan** as a necessary evil, produced at the request of a potential funder. They do not understand that a business plan is an essential management tool to set objectives for the business and monitor ongoing performance.

This is sometimes the difference between successful and unsuccessful firms. Those that succeed set adequate time to undertake the planning process enabling them to be proactive in their chosen market. Those that languish behind their competition spend a disproportionate amount of time being reactive, operating a fire-fighting approach.

There can be no doubt. Business planning should be undertaken by all businesses and the techniques used, no matter what size of firm, will remain basically the same.

As a pilot, before each flight I plan the route to my destination and the fuel that will be required. I cannot understand why a business owner fails to use the same analogy in charting the development of their business and the resources that they need to make the journey.

IS THIS YOU?

● *I've never written a business plan before and have no idea where to start.* ● *I cannot see why I should waste time writing a business plan when I know what I want to do and how I'm going to do it.* ● *I don't need to borrow money and anyway I don't want to tell anyone else what I'm planning to do.*

① UNDERSTANDING THE BUSINESS PLAN CONCEPT

A **business plan** is a written summary of what you hope to accomplish by being in business and how you will accomplish those objectives. It must contain clear goals and objectives with an explanation of how you intend to manage all of your resources, i.e. premises, equipment and staff, as well as finances, in order to achieve those goals and objectives.

A business plan should be seen as part of the planning process. It can never be complete because a number of factors can make it immediately out of date. These factors may include late payment by customers, or increased or unforeseen costs. The list is virtually endless.

For an existing business a good business plan should demonstrate that consideration has been given to the business's ongoing development. For a new business it must show that you have completed sufficient research and hold the necessary skills and vision to succeed.

Business owners should spend the equivalent of at least two weeks of their year planning. Most, however, actually spend less than two days each year on this vital task.

② UNDERSTANDING WHY YOU NEED A BUSINESS PLAN

A formal business plan should be seen as an important **management tool** by all businesses irrespective of size. It serves four critical functions:

- It helps to clarify, focus and research the development of the business.
- It provides a framework for the business strategy to be undertaken in order for the business to develop.
- The document can be used as a basis for discussion with third parties who have either a potential or an existing interest in the business such as shareholders, banks or other investors.
- It sets goals and objectives against which actual performance can be measured and reviewed.

If you are seeking external support, the business plan is probably the most important sales document you will ever produce. It gives the only opportunity to sell the concept behind your business and raise the funds to achieve success. Even if no external funding is required the whole planning process of thinking, discussing, researching, analysing and evaluating options will force you to understand more clearly what you want to achieve and how and when you will achieve it.

I have interviewed clients looking to raise funds for a business but who had not prepared even the most basic of business plans. While in some cases the basic business concept was good, insufficient thought had been put into the proposition. More often than not, the entrepreneur placed great emphasis on previous successful business ventures. They could not accept that this track record played only a small part in the decision whether to grant funding or not. The warning given regarding stock market investments is appropriate in this context: the past is not necessarily a guide to future performance.

(3) ESTABLISHING THE PURPOSE

The answer depends on the reason for writing the business plan and whether it is to be used internally within the business or exhibited externally.

Internal business plans are used solely within the business as a management tool and the intended recipients will be clearly defined. These could range from the sole use of the entrepreneur to set out clearly and succinctly their thoughts for the future, up to a department of a multinational company seeking approval for a new project. An internal business plan is easier to write because of the existing knowledge held by the recipient and as such less background information is required.

External business plans are usually written for three main reasons:

- to raise finance
- to value a business for either sale or purchase
- to find or retain a business partner, or establish a strategic alliance with another business.

External business plans will require considerable thought as to the intended **audience**. Three questions need to be answered:

- Who are the intended recipients?
- What will be their requirements?
- What language will they understand?

The majority of business plans are prepared by entrepreneurs seeking funding and as such a favourable first impression is all important. The preparation of a well-structured and comprehensive business plan will not in itself guarantee success, but the lack of a sound business plan will almost certainly ensure failure.

The **requirements of a potential funder** can be easily established. All of the main high street banks have specific business packs that outline the sort of content required in a business plan and you should study these carefully. The contents are required for a reason and if you miss a vital component in your business plan it merely shows the potential funder that you have not completed sufficient research. As a guide, a business plan template with suggested content is given in the Appendix.

Regarding the **language** that should be used, you may have a wonderful new business idea, but unless you can communicate your idea in words that are easily understood you are doomed to failure. This is covered in more detail in Chapter 5.

 KNOWING WHO TO INVOLVE

This question has two angles – internal assistance and external assistance in preparing the business plan. It also has a simple answer: **ownership**.

For any business plan to succeed it needs to be owned by all those who are required to carry out the actions outlined. This means in simple terms that if people do not believe in a plan from the outset they will not be committed to achieving the objectives and it will then surely fail.

On an **internal basis**, therefore, it is always preferable to gain input from those people best suited to providing the information required. For example, a Production Manager may be best suited to advising on production matters and a Sales Manager is probably best suited for advice on sales trends and competitor activity. The best solution is to involve all of those people who can bring expertise and knowledge to the overall business plan. Some owners balk at discussing their future plans with any of their staff on the basis that they want their ideas to be kept secret. This is a flawed argument. If the staff know what is being considered, and why, they can provide their own input to the business plan that may actually achieve a significantly better result.

On an **external basis** there is no shortfall of potential advisers and organisations who can help with a business plan. The important thing to remember again is ownership. An accountant can prepare all of the financial forecasts for you, and a management consultant can write a very nicely worded, smartly presented business plan, but is it **YOUR** plan, and, more importantly, do you actually understand it, and does it clearly set out **YOUR** aspirations for the business?

Time and time again I saw clients, with their accountants, and when it came to a discussion about the financial forecasts the client always deferred to the accountant. They could never understand my insistence that they should be able to answer my questions on the basis that the business was theirs, and therefore the financial forecasts represented their plans for the future. The plan is yours – make sure you own it.

 CONSIDERING CONFIDENTIALITY

For some business owners this can often be taken to the extreme as outlined above by even excluding those members of staff or management who could actually be of considerable benefit to the planning process. Realistically there are three options to take if you are concerned about confidentiality:

• Obtain a confidentiality agreement from anyone who is to see the business plan.

- Place a specific paragraph at the start of the business plan binding the reader to secrecy.
- Do not include sensitive information in the business plan.

The first option can range from a simple one-page letter to a full blown legal document although the latter are more commonly used in situations such as company takeovers. It will really depend on the circumstances. If you have any doubts on this aspect the advice of a commercial lawyer should be sought.

If you are submitting the business plan to a potential funder, such as high street bank, the inclusion of a paragraph binding the reader to secrecy serves no purpose whatsoever. They are already bound to keep the affairs of their customers confidential.

In a similar vein, if you avoid including sensitive information in the business plan, for example your cash flow forecast for the next twelve months, the whole business plan is of very little use to the potential funder. Without such information they will inevitably decline your proposition.

Overall there has to be a balance. You need to provide sufficient information to enable the recipient to analyse your plans and objectives. By the same token, if there is an element of commercial secrecy surrounding your venture, for example in the processes that you undertake in the course of manufacture, it is unlikely that the funder will wish to receive this information. As an example consider the case of Coca-Cola. The funders of this company have no idea what the actual ingredients are – this is a carefully guarded commercial secret.

MAKING WHAT MATTERS WORK FOR YOU

✓ Ensure your business plan includes clearly identifiable goals and objectives.

✓ You may only get one chance to sell your business concept to potential investors. Make sure you get it right first time.

✓ Make sure you understand the needs of your target audience and tailor your business plan accordingly.

✓ Involve the people around you to establish wide ownership of the business plan.

✓ Don't give away commercial secrets – but provide sufficient information to ensure the plan can be understood and evaluated by external funders and by those who will implement it.

2 Doing Your Research

*Inadequate research can only lead you down the
route to failure.*

**things that
really matter**

1 **USING A SWOT ANALYSIS**

2 **USING A PESTE ANALYSIS**

3 **FINDING OUT ABOUT YOUR COMPETITORS**

4 **CONSIDERING EXISTING RESOURCES**

5 **USING ANALYSIS OF PAST PERFORMANCE**

Adequate research is essential. Your business plan must
demonstrate to the reader that you have considered all the
influences that could impact upon your business. To do this
you must consider exactly what information you already
have and what research you need to undertake.

With an existing business, **internal research** is relatively
easy to undertake – although obviously impossible for a
new business. **External research**, on the other hand, can be
very thought provoking and there are a number of
management tools that you can utilise.

You also need to consider the different forms of research.
Primary research covers the investigations that you
undertake yourself and **secondary research** is the use of
information that has been obtained by a third party. An
example of secondary research would be the market
intelligence reports produced by specialist organisations such
as Mintel. Remember, research is defined as 'a systematic
investigation towards increasing the sum of knowledge'.
Better to have too much information than too little.

IS THIS YOU?

• I don't need to do any research. I know this business inside out. • There is nobody else doing the same thing so I have no competition. • I've no plans to export so the European market doesn't affect me. • I don't use technology so I'm not concerned at any new developments. • Financial analysis – sorry, you'll have to ask the accountant about that.

① USING A SWOT ANALYSIS

SWOT is the acronym for **strengths, weaknesses, opportunities and threats**. SWOT analysis makes you think about the positive sides of your existing or proposed business as well as the negative aspects.

Conducting a SWOT analysis is the construction of a non-financial balance sheet. Existing or potential assets are in the left columns representing the strengths and opportunities, and existing or potential liabilities are in the right columns representing the weaknesses and threats.

The analysis is undertaken using a grid (see page 17) to consider how you will match the strengths to the opportunities and how you will overcome the weaknesses and threats.

The key points to remember when using a SWOT analysis are:

- Build on strengths.
- Resolve weaknesses.
- Exploit opportunities.
- Avoid threats.

② USING A PESTE ANALYSIS

There are many factors in the **environment** that could

Strengths – something that you are doing right or are good at. It may be a skill, a competence or a competitive advantage that you have over rivals. Questions to ask: • What are your advantages? • What do you do well?	**Weaknesses** – something that you lack or do poorly when compared to rivals. A condition that puts you at a disadvantage. Questions to ask: • What could be improved? • What is done badly? • What should be avoided?
Opportunities – a realistic avenue for future growth in the business. Something to be used to develop a competitive advantage. Questions to ask: • What are the market trends? • How can they be exploited? • What chances are there for me?	**Threats** – a factor that you may or may not have control over that could lead to a decline in business. Questions to ask: • What obstacles do you face? • What is your competition doing? • What effect will increasing technology have?

impact upon your business and a **PESTE analysis** is designed to provide a focused framework for your research.

P – Political

E – Economic

S – Social

T – Technological

E – Environmental

• **Political forces** can have a direct impact on the way all businesses conduct their business; for example, health and safety legislation governing conditions in the workplace and consumer protection legislation covering labelling and packaging. Ensure that you identify and comply with all relevant legislation. Failure to do so can be extremely costly in terms of fines or penalties.

- **Economic forces** include the effects of inflation, interest rates and exchange rates. With the development of the Single European Market, even if you do not export any goods or services you may face increasing competition from firms within Europe. Consider carefully the economic trends within the UK. For example, if interest rates rise will this affect the spending habits of your customers? Can increased costs be passed on or is your market price-sensitive?

- **Social forces** include the consideration of changing demographic trends in your customer base and the changing social climate in parts of the country.

- **Technological forces** have been one of the most important aspects affecting businesses over the last decade. The development of information technology has affected the ways in which business is conducted; for example, the use of faxes and e-mail, quite apart from the opportunities now created by the Internet. You must consider the use of the latest available technology no matter what your field of business.

- The impact of a business on the **environment** must be considered as a separate issue. Some of the issues may overlap with the concerns relating to legislation but many – for example, the use of genetic engineering – are important enough to warrant an independent heading.

In summary, a PESTE analysis will provide you with a wider perspective on the **future** direction of your business. The keyword is 'future'. Unlike the SWOT analysis that concentrates on the present, PESTE analysis must be forward looking based on existing knowledge.

③ FINDING OUT ABOUT YOUR COMPETITORS

Many businesses insist they have no competition. This leads to three thoughts: either there are competitors they do not know, or there are genuinely no competitors, or there are no competitors because others have already tried and failed.

It is just as important to have all available information on your competitors as it is to have information on your own business. If you do not know what they are doing you cannot possibly hope to compete. Unless you are at the 'leading edge' of technology or innovation there will almost certainly be a competitor in the market somewhere. Remember, competition could potentially come from virtually anywhere in the world.

It is relatively easy to gain information about your competitors. They are in business to sell their products or services and therefore they need to provide information to potential customers. The following information should therefore be readily available by making telephone calls to your competitors:

- product range in terms of specification and price
- availability of discounts
- delivery arrangements
- terms of trade, i.e. cash or credit.

Information may already be available to you if you have an existing connection, or have been previously employed in the same industry. If you are a potential new entrant to the market, you may find that in conducting research into potential customers, some of these may be customers of your competitor. They may therefore be able to pass on information about the service they receive.

Once you have gained as much information as you can, a

SWOT analysis will put it into a logical form. Then you can assess how you will deal with your competitors' existing strengths and exploit their weaknesses.

 CONSIDERING EXISTING RESOURCES

Resources fall under four headings:

- **physical**: property, machinery and equipment
- **human**: number of people and required skills
- **financial**: cash management, debtor and creditor control
- **intangible**: brand names and company image.

A full audit of existing resources is necessary before you can consider what you will require for the future. Ask the following questions:

- What resources do I have already?
- How effective or efficient are they?
- How flexible are they?
- How balanced are they?
- Are any unnecessary or underutilised?

A simple list of resources is insufficient to consider whether they are adequate or indeed relevant to the future of your business. Consider the following questions under each resource sub-heading:

- **Physical** – are the premises sufficient for future expansion? How up to date is the machinery? Will it cope with expanding production?

- **Human** – what staff do we have? What are their skills? How adaptable are they to changing conditions?

- **Financial** – how good is our cash management? Do our customers pay on time? Do we pay our creditors on time?

- **Intangible** – what is our image like in the industry? Do we make the best use of business contacts? Do we have a good brand name?

⑤ USING ANALYSIS OF PAST PERFORMANCE

Many entrepreneurs have no idea how to use financial analysis. A basic understanding of the concept of financial analysis, and its limitations, can, however, be a valuable management tool in the business planning process.

This applies equally whether you are looking at your own business, or assessing your competition. If your competition is a limited company, you can obtain copies of their annual accounts from Companies House.

It never fails to amaze me how many entrepreneurs present forecasted figures that bear no resemblance to past performance, and can offer no real explanation as to how these can now be achieved.

There are a number of ratios that can be calculated from annual financial accounts. Examples include:

gross profit	– gross profit ÷ sales × 100
net profit	– net profit ÷ sales × 100
current	– current assets ÷ current liabilities
gearing	– total debt ÷ equity or owners' capital
stock turnover	– stock ÷ sales × 365
debtor payment period	– debtors ÷ sales × 365
creditor payment period	– creditors ÷ sales × 365

- **Gross** and **net profit** ratios are good indicators of rising costs, increasing overheads or discounted sales. An increasing ratio indicates improved profitability and a declining ratio reduced profitability.

- The **current** ratio relates to the liquidity of the business. If the resultant answer is less than 1, the business could be insolvent and without realising fixed assets, incapable of paying outstanding creditors.

- The **gearing** ratio measures the net worth of the business against the amount of borrowed funds. It is the amount of money invested in the business by the owners compared to the money invested by outside sources.

- The ratios for **stock turnover** and **debtor** and **creditor payment periods** will all be expressed as a number of days. **Stock turnover** indicates the number of days' stock that is held and should be realistic for the business concerned. For example, a business dealing in fresh produce should have a turnover of perhaps a few days at most.

- The ratios for **debtor** and **creditor payment periods** should relate to the terms of trade of the business. For example, a business that allows thirty days' credit should have a ratio of around the same figure. Any significant difference in the terms of trade and actual performance should be investigated.

You should also recognise that there are limitations in the use of ratios. To have any meaning whatsoever they should not be used in isolation but rather as comparisons of performance over a number of years. In this way they give an indication of the trends in business performance. They can then be used to set targets for the future and to monitor ongoing performance.

MAKING WHAT MATTERS WORK FOR YOU

✓ Use the SWOT analysis to build on strengths, resolve weaknesses, exploit opportunities and avoid threats.

✓ Use the PESTE analysis to provide a wider perspective on the future direction of your business.

✓ Gain as much information as possible on your competition to assess how you will deal with their strengths and exploit their weaknesses.

✓ Complete a full audit of all existing resources.

✓ Use ratio analysis to provide you with the financial trends within the business.

3 Evaluating All the Options

*Evaluating all available options is critical. Do not
overlook the obvious.*

1 ASSESSING YOUR OPTIONS

2 ARE THEY SUITABLE?

3 ASSESSING THEIR FEASIBILITY

4 ARE THEY ACCEPTABLE?

things that
really matter

The next step is to evaluate all the available options on the
basis of previously established business goals and objectives.
At the core of successful business planning lies a
comprehensive evaluation of the available options.

Assess all the available options using the analysis from
both the SWOT and PESTE research without relying on the
traditional methods that your business has previously used.
This also applies to a new business because there may be
long-established practices in the market that you can break
away from, thereby gaining competitive advantage.

*During the 1960s space race, NASA decided that it needed a writing
instrument that would work in the zero gravity confines of a space
capsule. Eventually a ball point pen was produced at a cost of
$241m. Russian astronauts used pencils to solve the same problem.*

Avoid resistance to change and preconceptions and evaluate
all the options that should contribute to the success of your
business. The four-stage process outlined below will help.

IS THIS YOU?

• I've done all the research but how do I evaluate all the options I have identified? • How do I select those options that will be best for me? • How do I use the SWOT analysis to evaluate these options? • Why should I look at new ideas?

① ASSESSING YOUR OPTIONS

Realistically there are five options available to any business. The first is to do nothing. This option should be avoided because it obviously achieves absolutely nothing.

The remaining four options are:

- Withdraw from the market entirely.
- Consolidate the existing position within the market.
- Increase market penetration.
- Introduce new products or services.

Withdrawing from the market can mean a number of options: complete liquidation of the business; a sale of the business to a competitor or a new management team; a licensing or sub-contracting agreement. The last option could arise if, for example, one part of the business was unprofitable on a stand-alone basis. However, if the work was to be sub-contracted it could make the overall business more economically viable.

Consolidation is usually an internal business option where, for example, the business may concentrate on improving quality, efficiency and productivity. All these actions would not necessarily increase the overall sales turnover, but they could have an effect on increased profitability.

Increasing market penetration would be an attempt to increase sales turnover by expanding into new markets for the existing products or services. This could be achieved by, for example, exporting abroad for the first time into new overseas markets. It could also include the potential takeover of similar competitors or collaboration with other businesses on joint ventures. This last option is becoming more and more popular, especially involving joint ventures with businesses within the European Market.

Introducing **new products and services** can be achieved in a number of ways. Within the business there may be substantial research and development opportunities for existing products or services that can be modified or extended so that they can be used in a different manner. Further options could include the takeover of businesses that offer alternative products, or you may be able to negotiate a licensing agreement to produce new products using your existing production capabilities.

The mere formulation of a problem is far more essential than its solution . . . to raise new questions, new possibilities, to regard old problems from a new angle requires creative imagination and marks real advances . . . (Albert Einstein)

 ARE THEY SUITABLE?

The suitability of a particular option can be measured by the extent to which it fits the needs of the business as identified using the SWOT analysis. Using the four key elements, the selected option should either:

- build on strengths
- resolve weaknesses
- exploit opportunities
- avoid threats.

For example, does this option capitalise on your business

strengths, overcome or avoid weaknesses or counter potential threats? Of prime importance, of course, is that it should fit in with your overall business objectives.

In some cases an option that is suitable is the only one that can be implemented despite reservations about whether it is feasible or acceptable. These do, however, usually involve declining businesses where the only option to ensure survival is downsizing with subsequent reductions in workforce levels.

During the early 1980s the survival of many top British companies, such as Jaguar and Lucas were in some doubt. The resultant options to ensure survival were indeed suitable, but to the workforce and unions, were neither feasible nor acceptable.

③ ASSESSING THEIR FEASIBILITY

An assessment of the feasibility of an option is primarily concerned with whether or not it can be implemented. For example, an option that seeks to break into a new market might be suitable in terms of achieving a perceived opportunity, but lack of resources could render it unfeasible.

At this stage of evaluating the available options there are a number of fundamental questions that need to be considered when assessing feasibility. Consider the following examples:

- Is this option capable of being funded? Does the business have sufficient internal resources, or, if outside funding is required, is this likely to be obtained?

- Can the business perform to the required level? Does the business have the capability of increasing productivity or quality standards?

- Can the necessary market position be achieved? Does

the business have sufficient marketing skills to increase sales turnover in potential new markets?

- Are the required skills available within the business? Do you have the required business skills to compete in new markets, or will additional staff resources be required? If new staff are required, where will they come from and what skills will they need?

- Can the necessary materials or services be obtained? Will the suppliers be able to meet the increased demand for raw material, and if so, on what terms will these be supplied?

These questions are only some examples of the sort of evaluation that should be undertaken when looking at the feasibility of the available options.

④ ARE THEY ACCEPTABLE?

The first question to be answered is to whom should these options be acceptable? The simple answer is that they have to be acceptable to the stakeholders within the business. There are many definitions of stakeholders, but in this instance they are considered to be the owners of the business together with potential or existing investors.

In many ways, while the suitability and feasibility may be uppermost in the minds of the owners of the business, if funding is being sought, it is of far greater importance that the chosen options are acceptable to the potential investors.

You should be under no illusions. Unless the selected options for the business are acceptable to potential investors they will not invest. The questions of suitability and feasibility are of secondary importance.

When considering options for acceptability give additional consideration to the following factors:

- The selected option must increase the profitability of the business. The reason for this is that if an outside investor is to consider investing, the business must generate additional income to pay for the investment in terms of either interest or dividends.

- The element of risk will be of prime importance to a prospective investor. They need to be convinced that the amount of risk they are taking by investing in the business is minimised and that not only will their investment be safe, but also they will receive a suitable reward.

- A key measure of the acceptability of an option is gained following an assessment of the returns that are likely to accrue to all stakeholders as a result of that option being adopted.

- Clearly define the capital structure of the business from the outset recognising the individual investment made by each party. This applies in all cases where there is more than one owner; for example, a new partner is being sought, or shares in a limited company are being offered in exchange for investment.

For some entrepreneurs, the question of relinquishing part ownership of their business is very emotive. In many cases there is a failure to recognise that by allowing an investor part ownership, the investor's commitment for the business to be a success can also increase. Part ownership of a thriving successful business is a better investment than total ownership and control of a failing business.

MAKING WHAT MATTERS WORK FOR YOU

✓ Understand the types of option available to you – withdraw, consolidate, expand or introduce new products or services.

✓ Use the SWOT and PESTE analysis to assess the suitability of an option. Does it build on a strength, resolve a weakness, exploit an opportunity, or avoid a threat?

✓ Assess the feasibility of an option by focusing on whether it can actually be implemented.

✓ When considering the acceptability of the option, concentrate on the requirements of all stakeholders in terms of balancing the risk against the reward.

4 Formulating the Strategy

Thinking is the hardest work there is, which is
probably the reason so few engage in it.
(Henry Ford)

4

things that
really matter

1 **DEFINING YOUR BUSINESS GOALS**

2 **CONSIDERING THE MARKETING STRATEGY**

3 **IDENTIFYING ANY ADDITIONAL RESOURCES**

4 **CONSTRUCTING THE FINANCIAL FORECASTS**

You are now ready to formulate your strategy, bringing
together all the initial objectives, refining them into a
logical format and preparing to write your business plan.

You need to start thinking about the overall structure of
the business plan. You also need to clearly define the goals
and objectives that may previously have been of a generalist
nature, setting clearly achievable targets. Consider also how
you will present the results of your research, and indeed,
what parts of that research you will include.

Writing the business plan may take a relatively short time,
but ensure that you allocate sufficient time for formulating the
underlying strategy. A business plan must be the result of a
careful and extensive research and development project and this
must be completed before words can be committed to paper.

Planning is an unnatural process, it is much more fun to do
something. The nicest thing about not planning is that failure comes
as a complete surprise rather than being preceded by a period of
worry and depression. (Sir John Harvey-Jones)

IS THIS YOU?

• I've done all the research and considered the available options. Where do I go now? • What criteria can I use to define the strategy? • Why is the marketing strategy so important? How can I identify what I need in terms of resources? • Surely the accountant will prepare the financial forecasts?

① DEFINING YOUR BUSINESS GOALS

Having outlined your initial objectives, by utilising the research you have undertaken and the evaluation of all available options, these objectives can now be redefined into targets for the business. One technique for drawing up these targets is to use the SMART criteria. **SMART** is an acronym for:

- **S**pecific
- **M**easurable
- **A**greed
- **R**ealistic
- **T**imed.

A crucial step in using the SMART criteria is being aware of how you aim to achieve your targets. As an example, consider the following hypothetical target for a distribution company:

> To improve the standard of customer service by reducing delivery times to an average of three days within the next twelve months. This will be achieved by the introduction of a new distribution system together with the use of new technology to track the stock and order systems.

As you can see, this target has all the components of the SMART criteria. It is quite specific, it is clearly measurable in terms of delivery days, it is agreed and realistic, and it is timed, the improvement to take place within twelve months. It is also clear how the target is to be achieved, i.e. with the use of new technology and a new distribution system.

② CONSIDERING THE MARKETING STRATEGY

The most difficult part of formulating your overall business strategy is the preparation of your marketing strategy. Without a successful marketing strategy your business will ultimately fail regardless of how good all the other parts of your business strategy are.

The subject of marketing is very wide ranging although in simplistic terms you need to consider the following headings when formulating your overall business strategy:

- customers and markets
- products or services
- pricing
- promotion
- place.

A clear understanding of **potential customers and markets** needs to be demonstrated. Who are you going to sell your products or services to and where are they situated? For example, are you looking at retail or wholesale sales? Are you aiming at individual customers in your locality? Are you aiming country- or world-wide?

You need to show exactly what **products and services** you are selling. Is it one product or service or are there many that will appeal to a wide range of different customers? Also consider product development. If a product or service has a limited shelf life, what will you need to do to ensure continued sales?

Pricing decisions can be difficult, especially if there are a number of competitors offering similar products or services. You need to take many factors into account when setting a price. In reality, there will probably never be a single 'right' price – the answer will fall within a price range. At one end will be the marginal cost of the product or service, below which it becomes unprofitable to produce and sell, and at the other end, the highest price that the market will tolerate.

Consider also the **expectation of the consumer**. In some cases the consumer may be prepared to pay a high price for a quality product, yet in other instances, the consumer is merely looking for the cheapest option.

One case that was unusual was a professional man offering a high quality service who found that he had set his price too low. The expectation of the consumer was for a high price and when they saw his price they assumed he was not very good. An increase in price to match the competition saw his workload soar.

The methods you will adopt for **promotion** also require careful thought. You must look at how and where your competitors advertise. You must establish a strategy to ensure that potential customers are aware of the products or services that you offer.

The question of **place** does not just relate to the physical location of the business but also to how and when the product or service will be offered for sale. For a service business, the question of location may be of little consequence, but for a retail business, for example, the question of correct location will be of prime importance.

In summary, your marketing strategy could make or break your business. Consumers will not necessarily beat a path to your door even if you do have the right product at the right price and in the right place. You must actively promote your business using all appropriate communication techniques to tell your customers how you will meet their needs.

③ IDENTIFYING ANY ADDITIONAL RESOURCES

Resources fall under four headings and you must consider them individually when you formulate your strategy:

- **physical**: property, machinery and equipment
- **human**: number of people and required skills
- **financial**: cash management, debtor and creditor control
- **intangible**: brand name and company image.

Successful formulation of your business strategy will almost certainly require changes in the resources available to your business. Having completed the audit of existing resources you will be aware of exactly what resources you already have at your disposal. Now you must establish what additional resources you will require.

Looking at **physical resources** first, you must decide whether the premises that you already have, or are proposing to use, will be sufficient to achieve your goals and objectives. You must also identify future machinery and equipment requirements.

Cost considerations will also need to be assessed using the evaluation techniques outlined previously. For example, it may not be feasible to purchase premises and so renting may be the only available option. Additionally, in terms of machinery and equipment, suitable options could include outright purchase, hire purchase or leasing.

It is not necessary to take a final decision on purchase options but comparable figures must be available for assessment when the financial projections for your strategy are produced.

Regarding **human resources**, you are already aware of the people you employ and the skills that they possess. Will they, however, fit in with your proposed strategy and if not, can they be trained or will additional, or indeed replacement, staff be required? For a new business you will need to establish the people required and the skills that they should possess.

Management skills must be considered. As a small business grows many entrepreneurs find themselves having to deal with tasks that they are not suitably qualified to deal with. For example, you may find that you are spending a disproportionate amount of time dealing with administration when you should be dealing with customers.

Under these circumstances an assistant who is capable of dealing with the routine administration could be extremely useful. They could probably be financed by the additional sales that would be achieved when you are doing what you do best. You must consider your own role in the business, and clearly define your responsibilities.

In terms of **financial resources**, you will already know what resources are at your disposal and how the business is performing. The question, however, of what additional finance will be required cannot be answered in full until the financial projections have been completed. What can be established at this stage is the additional financial resources that you may be prepared to invest, and indeed, the surplus financial resources already available within your business.

For a new business it is important to have a **unique image**, whether this just includes a basic logo design on stationery or a fully co-ordinated image on all vehicles, uniforms for employees and product packaging. While brand and image are **intangible resources**, they require the same degree of thought.

 **CONSTRUCTING THE FINANCIAL FORECASTS**

Let me make it clear that I do not consider that you should draw up the financial forecasts yourself. These must be done by a qualified accountant to ensure that the effects of VAT and other statutory payments such as National Insurance and income tax are taken into account.

What you must do is ensure that the original base figures for the financial forecasts have been prepared by you as the entrepreneur. You need to be able to understand these figures because it is your business. Ultimately you will need to track the financial performance against the forecasts and take corrective action where necessary.

As I have already outlined, there may be many possible financial options that are available. While you can use the expertise of your accountant in modelling the various forecasts, you need to take the final decision as to the suitability, feasibility and acceptability of these financial forecasts. You must also understand the basic assumptions that are incorporated into these forecasts.

Ownership is the keyword. The business plan is yours, together with all the content including the financial forecasts, and you need to have a total understanding of what they reveal, even if they have been produced by your accountant.

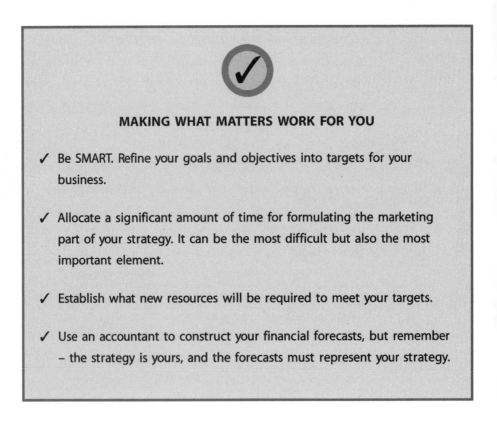

MAKING WHAT MATTERS WORK FOR YOU

✓ Be SMART. Refine your goals and objectives into targets for your business.

✓ Allocate a significant amount of time for formulating the marketing part of your strategy. It can be the most difficult but also the most important element.

✓ Establish what new resources will be required to meet your targets.

✓ Use an accountant to construct your financial forecasts, but remember – the strategy is yours, and the forecasts must represent your strategy.

5 Constructing the Business Plan

Constructing a business plan is like making a model from a kit. All the small components are fixed together to make a nicely finished product.

6 things that really matter

1 **THE ALL-IMPORTANT SYNOPSIS**

2 **KEEPING IT SIMPLE**

3 **USING FACT NOT FICTION**

4 **TELLING THE TRUTH**

5 **WHAT TO INCLUDE**

6 **WHAT NOT TO INCLUDE**

The preparation of a written business plan is not the end result of the planning process. Achieving the objectives outlined in the plan is your ultimate aim but the writing is an important intermediate stage. For an established business it demonstrates that the development of the business has been carefully considered and, for a start-up business, it demonstrates thorough research of the potential market.

No two business plans will be identical – they must be tailored to meet the individual situation. However, most business plans follow a tried and tested structure with sub-headings to cover all eventualities. See the Appendix for a sample business plan template, with content guidance.

Your business plan is a guide to where you are now, where you want to get to, and how you will get there.

Many business plans that I have seen have not been very good, making no attempt to pre-empt any obvious questions that I would have and presenting lots of mainly irrelevant information. There was no clear strategy on how the goals and objectives would be achieved.

IS THIS YOU?

● *I've never written anything like this before. Where do I start?* ● *I've completed vast amounts of relevant research, surely I should include it all in the plan?* ● *Why is the synopsis so important?* ● *Why do I need one if all the information is in the plan?*

① THE ALL-IMPORTANT SYNOPSIS

Although the marketing section of your business plan is the most important part to you, to the reader of your plan the **synopsis** will be the most important.

This could be your one chance to make a favourable impression on your target audience. Do not waste it. The synopsis must contain sufficient information in a concise format to make your audience want to discover more about your plans. The synopsis should not normally be longer than one page and it should contain the following information:

● the background to your business or your business idea
● an outline of your proposals
● what you need from your audience.

This final part is very important. If you are putting a proposal to a potential funder you must tell them what it is you want and how it will be repaid. While this will be covered in detail in the body of the business plan, a brief summary needs to be clearly outlined.

Because the synopsis is supposed to be a summary of the entire business plan, you should complete all other sections before you attempt to write this section.

Many business plans arrived with no synopsis of the content. Even if they did have one it was usually inadequate and did not tell me what was required from me. In some cases there was no coherent structure at all, and with pressure on my time, these were declined.

② KEEPING IT SIMPLE

Entrepreneurs sometimes get so mixed up in jargon that they forget that someone outside their industry may have no idea what they are talking about. When writing your business plan you must avoid the use of jargon, or, where it cannot be avoided, give a clear explanation of what it actually means.

Consider these two theoretical projects that I was asked to assess for potential funding:

● An accredited crystalline anthropoid homologue – a solar-recyclable compacted aqueous transitional-state hominid isomorph assembled as a juvenile peer-bonding mechanism.

● A dual carbohydrate-oxidation chamber – an electroresistive self-limiting Maillard reaction initiator for infrared irradiative thermal preparation of microbially aerated, kiln-stabilised milled cereal-endosperm sections.

Which would you consider funding? If you chose the first example your money would literally have been thrown down the drain – you funded the building of a snowman. If you chose the second you would have least have invested wisely – you funded the production of a two-slice toaster.

These two examples demonstrate the importance of keeping the business plan content simple. If your target audience has no idea what you are talking about they are unlikely to seek an explanation. They will merely refuse to assist.

You can have brilliant ideas, but if you can't get them across, your ideas won't get you anywhere. (Lee Iacocca)

③ USING FACT NOT FICTION

When you completed your research you will have discovered numerous facts and figures. You will also no doubt have unearthed the opinions and assertions of many people. The important part now is to sort fact from fiction.

Within your business plan you will make a number of assumptions, not just relating to the financial forecasts, and it is important that you support these assumptions with facts. The target audience for your business plan needs to be convinced that what you are telling them is true. You must present them with firm evidence.

Avoid waffle and unsubstantiated claims. For example, describing your target market as 'increasing substantially year on year' means very little. If you are going to make a claim such as this then back it up with hard facts and evidence. For example, 'the market has increased from £Xm to £Ym over the last two years. According to research carried out by Anytown University, growth will continue at a rate of Z% per annum for the foreseeable future.'

This demonstrates to your target audience that you have done your research, understood the results and converted this information into an opportunity for your business. Remember, if the target audience is sufficiently interested in your business plan they may well do some research of their own in order to substantiate your claims. You need to make sure that the facts that they obtain match your own.

④ TELLING THE TRUTH

Always tell the truth. The importance of your integrity and reputation as an entrepreneur is vital. If you misrepresent the facts, or even worse, lie about any part of your background or your business history, you will lose the confidence and trust of potential or existing funders.

In some circumstances you could even face personal liability despite operating your business under the auspices of a limited liability company.

If you fail to provide information that is relevant to your business proposal this could be seen as blatant misrepresentation. Even if this fact is not discovered until some time later the damage will have been done.

The funder will not simply forget the event on the basis that as they have already invested they will stay with you. You will have lost their trust and this will never be regained. Once the funds that have been invested are repaid, or when you require new funding, the simple answer will be 'no'.

A lie gets halfway round the world before the truth has a chance to get its pants on. (Sir Winston Churchill)

(5) **WHAT TO INCLUDE**

Once you have concluded your research you must refine the information for inclusion in your business plan.

- Remember that your business plan must answer your potential funders' questions. It should be presented in an easy-to-read and logical format to convince your target audience that you know what you are talking about.

- Put yourself in the position of the potential funder. You know the sort of questions you asked yourself when doing your research and compiling the SWOT and PESTE analyses. Ensure that the business plan answers all these questions.

- A potential funder will not be impressed if they have a question that you are unable to answer. All that this demonstrates to them is that your research is inadequate and based on this fact alone they may simply decline your proposition. As I have said previously, you may only get one chance, so get it right first time.

- Finally, check and double check that both the words and figures in your financial forecasts match. For example, if the business plan states that growth in profitability of X% in the first year will be achieved, make sure that your forecasts actually show this growth.

Many times I saw business plans that had obviously been completed by two separate parties. The entrepreneur had written the text and the accountant had compiled the figures. This in itself was not a problem but when the words and figures did not match there was little point in reading any further. The financial information was obviously incorrect and therefore the repayment programme for the proposed borrowing was in doubt.

 ## WHAT NOT TO INCLUDE

Sometimes it is difficult to decide exactly what should and what should not be included in a business plan. It is important to remember that, while it needs to be concise, it also needs to be clear and uncluttered. Including irrelevant material can make the plan very difficult to read and this will not help your cause.

- For example, as part of your research you may have completed a customer survey. Do not include all the answer sheets in the plan, but do include a brief summary of your analysis.

- As another example, you may have obtained secondary research from a company such as Mintel giving details of the exact market conditions. Do not include the actual document, but make reference to the findings in summarised format. If the target audience requires sight of the research they will ask for it.

In essence, be selective about what you include in your business plan. If you include reams of paper that make the plan difficult to read or understand, you face the risk of a potential funder losing interest. You must capture their attention so that they want to read further.

MAKING WHAT MATTERS WORK FOR YOU

✓ Make sure the synopsis is concise and captures the reader's attention.

✓ Avoid the use of jargon.

✓ Make sure that your business plan is factually correct and support your claims with suitable evidence.

✓ Always tell the truth. Your integrity and reputation as an entrepreneur should never be placed in any doubt.

✓ Make sure that the content of the plan answers all the potential questions your target audience is likely to ask.

✓ Don't clutter up the plan with irrelevant material.

6 Review and Start the Process Again

The process of planning does not stop with the production of the business plan. Constant review is necessary to stay ahead of the competition.

things that really matter

1 **REVIEWING PERFORMANCE AGAINST BUDGETS**

2 **MANAGING RISK**

3 **MANAGEMENT INFORMATION**

4 **STAYING AHEAD OF THE COMPETITION**

Congratulations! You have completed your business plan and raised the finance for your business. However, that is not the end of your business plan. It was written to chart the development of your business over a defined period of time. This is merely the start of your journey and you need to take steps to monitor your ongoing progress along the route. You must also consider the possibility that some aspects of your business plan could go wrong.

As part of their agreement to fund your business, some lenders may insist upon the production of regular financial information. Even if they do not, if you are astute you will recognise that this is something you should have in any event. You need to keep track of your ongoing performance to ensure that your overall targets will be met.

The way to succeed in business is to constantly review and amend your plan in the light of actual, as opposed to budgeted, performance. The process of business planning is a continuous cycle and does not stop with the construction of a business plan.

IS THIS YOU?

● I've finished my business plan and have succeeded in raising the finance I needed, so that's it, isn't it? ● I don't see the point in constantly reviewing the plan. I've set all the goals and objectives, now I need to just get on with it. ● What have risk analysis and contingency planning got to do with me? ● A Management Information System – that sounds too technical for me. ● I've already assessed the competition and they don't pose any threat.

① REVIEWING PERFORMANCE AGAINST BUDGETS

There is no point in setting goals and objectives within your business plan unless you monitor how you are performing. Unfortunately, most entrepreneurs do not undertake any form of review and only react in the light of a problem. Take the time and trouble to monitor your business and you may avoid problems before they actually occur.

Reviewing performance applies to all aspects of the business and not just to the financial side. While it is relatively easy to track financial performance it is more difficult to review non-financial performance that could actually be the cause of a variance in the financial performance.

For example, a monthly sales budget can be easily compared to the actual sales receipts for the month. How do you establish the cause when, for example, the actual sales figure is less than projected? This is where non-financial information is vital. The lack of sales could be related to either an internal or an external problem.

- An internal problem, for example, might be that a piece of machinery used in production has been subject to numerous breakdowns. This would mean that actual production targets to meet the projected sales could not be achieved due to the lack of finished products.

- An external problem is normally something that the business has no control over; for example, a postal strike.

In both cases you need to take action at an early stage to counter the prospective threat to your business. Without regular review these problems could become insurmountable with the potential for substantial loss of profits, or in the extreme, even business failure.

Invariably when reviewing the banking facilities available to a customer the business plan had been forgotten. Despite the projection that the overdraft would be repaid it was still required although the customer could not see the problem. In far too many cases this was simply evidence of losses being made.

 MANAGING RISK

The secret to success is to **minimise the effect of risks** upon your business and the only way to achieve this is through **contingency planning**.

Risks are usually associated with crises that take two forms – internal and external. Examples of an **internal crisis** include power or machinery failure or even something as simple as losing your briefcase. An **external crisis** could include bad debts or the more extreme examples of fire or flood.

You need to consider a number of key components when making contingency plans:

- identifying the potential crises that could affect your business
- gathering information about the potential causes and effects of such a crisis

- deciding the actions to be taken in the event of such a crisis.

To identify potential crises that could affect your business you will need to draw up a **crisis audit**. In order to do this you should involve all members of staff because they will have detailed knowledge of any potential problems that could occur in their individual jobs. At this stage do not consider the seriousness of a potential crisis because small problems can become large problems if not dealt with correctly from the outset.

You then need information on the likely causes of each crisis and how it will affect your business.

- For example, consider the risks involved with only having one supplier for essential components that you use in a manufacturing process. If they ceased trading what effect would that have on your business? How quickly could you find an alternative supplier?

Finally, draw up a formal contingency plan that can be referred to in the event of a crisis.

- Using the example quoted above, this would contain the names and contact details of alternative suppliers. A better method of countering the risk used in this example, however, would be to spread the risk. Even if only small quantities are involved, use more than one supplier from the outset.

③ MANAGEMENT INFORMATION

Management information comes in a variety of formats. One of the most important are monthly financial accounts that allow you to compare your budgeted forecasts with your actual performance.

Apart from financial information you also need management information on the other resources within your business. For example, is your machinery operating at the optimal level? Are your staff performing as they should? A **Management Information System** must be an entirely distinct part of your business and time and resources should be allocated to ensure that it is effective.

- You must prioritise the information within the Management Information System in order to keep the system workable. There is little point in keeping track of information if you have no idea of how you will use that information in the future.

- Decide what information is crucial to oversee your business operation and then only store appropriate information that will meet that objective. The simpler the system, the more likely it will succeed.

- Finally, take the time to explain the purpose of the system to your staff and seek their help in design and implementation. If you keep your staff in the dark this will more than likely cause a reduction in morale leading to possible operational problems and a downturn in productivity.

④ STAYING AHEAD OF THE COMPETITION

Ongoing market intelligence and competitor information are vital. Up-to-date information about your market will keep you aware of changes or developments that could affect your business. This information may also indicate trends in consumer demand that you can exploit. It could also potentially help you identify economic trends in the market that could affect the buying habits of your customers.

- Market intelligence will enable you to update your **sales forecasts** on a regular basis and this will also help you to review your overall strategy.

- You should also maintain statistics on which form of **advertising** is bringing you customers in order to achieve optimum value for money.

- It is also important that you keep track of your **competitors**. You need to find out on an ongoing basis what they are doing, what they are charging, and any new products that they have launched which could compete with you.

- If you employ sales staff, make sure that they obtain **feedback from your customers**. It is more than likely that your customers will also be looking at the activities of your competitors and it may be that they can provide you with 'inside' information. For example, it is not unknown for a competitor to approach a customer of a rival and offer some form of inducement such as a discount or better credit terms in order to gain their business. Unless you have information on this sort of activity at an early stage you could well find your customer base declining.

Competitive advantage is everything in business. You must retain a **unique selling point** that will consistently bring you new customers as well as repeat business. The only way that you can do this is to continually research the market to establish what is happening.

Business more than any other occupation is a continual dealing with the future. It is a continual calculation, an instinctive exercise in foresight. (Henry R. Luce)

MAKING WHAT MATTERS WORK FOR YOU

✓ Review the performance of your business on a regular basis. The construction and success of your business plan does not signal the end of the planning process.

✓ Minimise the risks to your business by contingency planning. Analyse the potential crises that could affect you and plan in advance to deal with them.

✓ Introduce a suitable Management Information System to track the performance of your business and the use of available resources. Be sensitive how you use it and, above all, keep it simple.

✓ Maintain a competitive advantage. Compile ongoing research on your competitors and stay ahead of the field.

Appendix A: Sample Business Plan Template

CONTACT DETAILS

This should be no more than a single page with details of the company or trading name, the registered and trading address and contact name with telephone and fax numbers.

It should also contain details of any advisers that may have assisted you such as your accountant or solicitor.

SYNOPSIS

A short synopsis of the business plan should be given, usually no more than one page. Make the reader aware from the outset exactly what the plan is all about, what it has been written for, and what is being sought. If seeking funding, state exactly how much, for what, and how long it will take to repay.

This section of the business plan should be written last.

BUSINESS BACKGROUND AND HISTORY

If the reader has no knowledge of the business, make sure that a full background and history are provided. This should cover when the business was started and how it has developed together with any significant milestones or achievements. Details should also be given of any accreditation gained such as quality standard awards or awards from industry or other bodies.

If, as in the case of a new business, there is no background history then the plan needs to include details of why the business is starting up and short details of the owner's own background and experience.

Do not include too much information on this final aspect as this will be covered in a later section.

THE PRODUCT

Give a precise description of exactly what products or services the business will be offering.

Outline clearly what the products or services will do for the consumer, and what competitive advantages these offer to differentiate them from those that may already be available in the market.

OPERATIONAL PROCESS

This section is only appropriate to a firm that is involved in direct manufacturing of a product.

If appropriate give full details of the exact procedures required from the basic ordering of raw materials right through all the production stages to achieving the final finished product.

Do not use any jargon and make sure that, while the production process is explained exactly, keep it simple. If the process is long and complicated involving numerous production stages, then merely use a flow diagram and bullet points.

MARKET ANALYSIS

This is one of the most important sections of the business plan because it deals with the overall market and should establish exactly how the business specifically operates in that market. Details should therefore be given of:

- the overall size of the market, both domestic and international

- trends within that market – supported by relevant figures

- specific details of direct competitors – who they are, what they do and how they compare

- market segmentation in terms of trade, retail, wholesale and mail order

- pricing expectations

- potential customers

- quality and service standards

- relevant legislation such as Health and Safety

- environmental concerns

- relevant independent market research information if available.

This can never be an exhaustive list and each business plan will require differing market analysis depending on the market in which the business operates.

MARKETING STRATEGY

Following the market analysis you can now start to formulate the marketing strategy and the initial stage will probably involve the use of a SWOT analysis.

This will set out in a logical manner the strengths, weaknesses, opportunities and threats and while this may not be used in the actual business plan, it will assist in formulating the marketing strategy around the five key components:

- **Customers and markets** – a clear understanding of the potential customers and markets needs to be shown. In other words, whom are you going to sell your products or services to?

- **Product** – what it is that the business will sell. Remember this has been covered previously and therefore only a brief description is necessary with comparisons to any existing products gleaned from the analysis.

- **Price** – how much will be charged and how this figure has been calculated. How does it compare to the competition and what sort of margin or mark-up has been used and why?

- **Promotion** – how will the business advertise its product or service and where. How much will it cost and over what period, i.e. will there be a large product launch campaign followed by smaller adverts in the following time periods?

- **Place** – where will the business operate from and why. How will the products be distributed and where will they be sold?

It is vitally important that the business achieves what is known as the correct 'marketing mix' within the strategy with all components correctly balanced. As an example, there is little point in trying to sell the product on a pure price basis when the market research that you carried out for the market analysis tells you that customers are looking for a high quality product.

THE PROJECT

This section should give a short synopsis of the project that will in effect summarise the next few sections.

Details should be given of the reasons behind the project, exactly what it is and what benefits it will bring to the business such as cost savings. In addition, summarised details of job creation and capital expenditure should be outlined.

Most importantly of all, set out the finance required and exactly what that funding will be used for, i.e. working capital in terms of revenue expenditure or fixed capital for expenditure on assets such as premises and equipment.

As with the synopsis, this section is best left until all other parts of the business plan have been put together.

MANAGEMENT STRUCTURE

Where there are only a limited number of key personnel, as in the case of sole traders or small partnerships, a full background profile should be inserted here for every member of the management team.

For larger organisations it is necessary to include a full management structure diagram clearly showing levels of responsibility and reporting lines.

In all cases, full details of all members of the management team should be given which clearly show the experience and skills that they bring to the business. In the case of any anticipated new members of the team, define exactly what skills will be necessary to do the job and state whether there is anyone in mind to fill the position.

HUMAN RESOURCES

Set out in table format all staff presently employed together with projections for the required levels of staff over the next three years.

Where additional staff are required for the expansion of the business, give details of specific responsibilities and potential salary or wage. If the new members of staff are required in the short term, say what efforts have been made to recruit or indeed if there is already a potential candidate.

PREMISES AND EQUIPMENT

For an existing business, give exact details of the present trading premises in terms of freehold or leasehold or rented with details of monthly or annual rental payments, length of lease, review dates and possible market valuation.

For new businesses, give details of proposed location and, as above, whether freehold, leasehold or rented, rental payments, proposed length of lease and likely start date.

Details of capital expenditure should also be given in table format for all equipment to be purchased over the life of the business plan, usually three years. If relevant, reasons for such purchases should be given especially where such new equipment will bring about cost savings or greater operational efficiency.

FINANCIAL INFORMATION

Provide summarised tables of the business's previous financial performance and of the forecasted cash flow, profit and loss and balance sheets in order that comparisons can be seen in a simple logical format.

It is also useful to provide summarised accounting ratios for comparison purposes; for example, gross and net profit, gearing and liquidity.

If the business is involved in importing or exporting, full details in terms of percentage sales and purchases should be given.

In the case of separate groups of products or services, these should be split as far as possible with specific details of percentage sales and related direct costs.

FUNDING REQUIREMENT

Set out details of existing finance available such as bank overdrafts and specific details of the new finance being sought in terms of type of funding, i.e. bank loan or increased overdraft, hire purchase, leasing, or equity via either venture capital or business angel.

Also set out the existing capital structure of the business in terms of issued share capital or owner's capital and whether this is to be charged.

In the case of a new start business, details should also be given of the opening capital to be injected, and if relevant, the source of that injection whether in terms of cash or introduction of assets.

Finally, set out the timing and source of repayment, usually in terms of retained profits as evidenced by the profit and loss forecasts, or less frequently, in the case of equity capital provided by venture capitalists, the anticipated stock flotation timetable.

RISK EVALUATION

The final section should contain a sensitivity analysis. This must look at what may happen in the event of variations in the business plan forecasts and what could be done to minimise the risk both to the business and to the potential funders.

This must clearly demonstrate that all possible risks have been considered, such as a downturn in overall turnover or a reduced overall profit margin due to increased costs. Within the business plan you need to show that you have allowed for such risks with contingency strategies.

Appendix B:
Useful Contacts

Business Links provide a wide range of information useful to the small and medium sized business. For your nearest office call: (0345) 567 765.

British Chambers of Commerce
Manning House
22 Carlisle Place
London SW1P 1JA
Tel: (020) 7565 2000. Fax: (020) 7565 2049

British Library Business Information Research Service
25 Southampton Buildings
London WC2A 1AW
Tel: (020) 7412 7457. Fax: (020) 7412 7453

Business and Innovation Centres (Head Office)
Aston Science Park, Love Lane
Aston Triangle
Birmingham
West Midlands B7 4BJ
e-mail: ebnbhambic@attmail.com
Website: www.astonsciencepark.co.uk
Tel: (0121) 359 0981. Fax: (0121) 359 0433

Companies House
Crown Way
Maindy
Cardiff
South Glamorgan CF4 3UZ
Tel: (029) 2038 8588. Fax: (029) 2038 0900

Department of Trade and Industry
Management Best Practice Directorate
4th Floor
1 Victoria Street
London SW1H 0ET
Website: http://www.dti.gov.uk/mbp/
Tel: (020) 7215 5000

The Environment Agency (Head Office)
Rio House
Waterside Drive
Aztec West
Almondsbury
Bristol BS32 4UD
Website: www.environment-agency.gov.uk
Tel: (0645) 333 111. Fax: (01454) 624 409

Office for National Statistics
(Population, Health and Social Statistics)
1 Drummond Gate
London SW1V 2QQ
e-mail: info@ons.gov.uk
Tel: (020) 7533 6260. Fax: (020) 7533 6261

Office for National Statistics
(Economic and Business Statistics)
Government Buildings
Cardiff Road
Newport
Gwent NP9 1XG
e-mail: library@ons.gov.uk
Tel: (01633) 812 973. Fax: (01633) 812 599

Mintel International Group Ltd
18–19 Long Lane
London EC1A 9HE
e-mail: enquiries@mintel.co.uk
Tel: (020) 7606 6000. Fax: (020) 7606 5932

National Federation of Enterprise Agencies
Trinity Gardens
9–11 Bromham Road
Bedford MK40 2UQ
Tel: (01234) 354 055

Reuters Business Briefings
85 Fleet Street
London EC4P 4AJ
Tel: (020) 7250 1122. Fax: (020) 7324 4527

Sources of Unofficial UK Statistics
Gower Publishing Limited
Gower House
Croft Road
Aldershot
Hampshire GU11 3HR
Tel: (01252) 331 551. Fax: (01252) 344 405

Phil Stone
Parkstone Management Consultancy
http://www.pkstone.demon.co.uk